In Search of Love

In Search of Love

Sarah Hamilton

To order additional copies of this book, contact:
Xlibris Corporation
0800-891-366
www.xlibris.co.nz
Orders@Xlibris.co.nz
700287

INTRODUCTION

This is a true and honest story of my life and what has happened. It has been very hard, and I thought I would not get there at times. But I kept fighting through and have come out of it the other side, and now being able to enjoy life within reason has made it all worth it. It is very close to my heart, and I feel so strongly that there are so many other women in this same kind of abusive situation and are trapped and scared to do anything about it. If I can help other women to see the truth and give courage to remove themselves from an abusive relationship, which also means being dominated and bullied as well as being beaten, and to be able to move on for a free life, well then I will be very happy.

It is hard to move away and break the cycle, but it is so worth it in the end for happiness, well-being, and sanity. It also enables children to be children again. So I hope this book can give people courage to stand on their own two feet and walk tall. And see the light at the end of the tunnel. You can do anything if you put your mind to it. And I have to say that it's the best thing I have ever done with no regrets, and you can do this too; you deserve a life free from any animosity. So please read this and let it give you courage to move on.

In Search of Love
Living Before and after with a Narcissist.
Surviving an Abusive life

CHAPTER 1

The next morning, I woke with my sore head on my bloodied pillow. I ran my fingers across my face. I had a swollen eye and split lips. I ran to the bathroom, and I saw I had bruises down both side of my cheeks, right down to my chin. My dad had beaten me, and I really do not know what for. I felt very sore and very anxious to go downstairs. And it hit me like a ton of bricks. How could my dad do this to me? It had taken all my love and respect away for this man and made me realise that he is a complete monster. My stomach ached, and I felt sick and knotted with disbelief and hurt. My head felt so sore and was so swollen that I could hardly open my eyes. I cried as I couldn't understand how my dad could do this to me. 'What am I going to do? How am I going to cope?'

After I had pulled myself together, I went downstairs to find my mum drinking a cup of tea. She just stared at me and said, 'Well, it's obvious you can't go to school till the bruises have gone.' So I was off school for nearly two weeks. My dad came home that night and did not even look or speak to me; he just carried on as though nothing had happened. How could he? Over the next three weeks, my face slowly healed; my face went all bright colours from red, purple, black, brown, and yellow. I was sad, scared, and disappointed as I realised that my parents were not the usual kind, loving parents. My dad was violent with a very nasty temper, and my mum was too gutless to do or say anything to protect us kids. How could my mum just calmly take it, when she should be protecting me and doing something about it? Loving me would have been nice, but no that was too difficult. I made a huge decision then. 'I am leaving as soon as I am able and going to sort my own life out without them as they are no use to me.' My other brother and sisters just kept their heads down and did everything my dad commanded so as not to set him off again.

I had two sisters and one brother. Unfortunately, it was only me that my dad used to knock around. I grew up hating him and waiting on the time I could leave home. Neither parent showed us love, so we all survived by looking out for each other. I was only eleven when my dad had done this, so I had a few years to wait till I was free. But I was determined. I had my whole life ahead of me, and it was not going to be ruined by this bully. Also I remember that mealtimes were the worst. We all had to sit round the table as a family every night, which was fine, but I had to sit next to my dad and he was the world's worst eaters I had ever seen. He would chomp and eat with his mouth open, making these awful noises loudly, so much so that I could not stand it. If I tutted, he would smack me across the face, hitting my ears. Sometimes I would sit there with my finger in my ear, trying to block out the noise, but if he saw what I was doing, he would smack me again round the ears. I couldn't win; it was horrid. So as soon as I could and was old enough, I used to make excuses not to be there for meals.

Two years had passed with the odd thing and another. The normal abuse would still carry on, and I just keep telling myself, 'Hang on in there. You will be free from this soon.' That's what kept me going. But I was mortified to think that my parents were the way they were and not like a normal loving family.

One day I was on my way home from school alone; I went to walk past the park gates that were close to our home, when a man came out and took my hand. There was no one about for me to call to. 'What shall I do? If I run, he will catch me. He has hold of my hand, and there is no one about. There is nothing I can do,' I thought, so I reluctantly, quietly walked alongside him. He took me to the men's toilets that were in the middle of the park, and he sexually abused me. With some sufficient force, I struggled and managed to get free eventually, so I ran home scared stiff, expecting my parents to give me the love and support that I needed. My mum just sat quietly in the chair, while my dad said that we had better call the police. He was looking at me as though it was my fault. What a bastard my own dad saying that; I felt so empty and alone. After a phone call to the police, they requested that we go down to the station to make a statement, which my dad did. That was so embarrassing and undignified, but I had to do it.

The police were very nice, I must say—more supportive than my parents were. Because this man had done more to me than first thought, I had to go to the hospital for an examination. My dad took me down; by this time the newspapers had been told of this and were at the hospital, waiting to speak with my dad. I was led there, very scared, alone, and hurt by being sexually abused, but instead of my dad loving and supporting me, he thrived in all the publicity and attention and the feeling of importance. Here was my dad having a daughter sexually abused, and all he could do was think of himself and practically bragging that this had happened. And he sat there, wallowing in self-importance. By this time, I was numb, and so, so hurt and couldn't believe how callous my parents could be. What a life? I just didn't want to be here any more. If this is what life had to offer, well then I ought to give up now. Because I lived in a very small town then, news travelled very fast, and everyone got to hear about it. So if I was walking through the town, people would stare at me. You could see them whisper to each other. It was awful. I will never forget it, and that haunts me to this day. So if my dad walked through the town, people would stop him and talk to him about it and he would proudly stand there as though he were the king and discuss it in public. He thrived on everyone's concern. That just made me feel sick. How could he?

After a short time, they found the man, arrested him, and charged him with rape. After his court case, he got sentenced to three years in jail, which in my eyes was not long enough. But everyone just carried on as though it never happened, and I was left in a stewed-up state. My mum and dad were not sympathetic at all, and that was something I had to leave on my shoulders and carry around with me.

A short time passed, and I was walking home from school and someone shouted at me. I looked across to see a man standing in a gateway, showing me all his private parts. I rushed home again to tell my parents. My mum couldn't be bothered to even talk to me, and my dad blamed me, saying, 'God knows what you are doing to always have this happen to you.' We had to go to the police station again to make a statement, and I will always remember as they joked with me, saying I would have to have my own mug shortly if I keep having this happen. I did think to myself, 'God, why me? What am I doing? Is this always going to happen? If so, I don't want to be here.' But I had to carry on.

My dad used to play table tennis for the county. He encouraged me to do it too, and I was really good at it. I eventually ended up playing for the county and everyone wanted me to play for them, *but* I was doing something I didn't want to do. And my dad was forcing me to do something I didn't want to do. So I tried to play badly on purpose so that I wouldn't be made to do something I didn't want to, 'cause every Monday evening, I had to play and participate in front of lot of people that I didn't want to. But I also realised that being with my dad, you didn't have much of a choice. My dad kept forcing me to play and wasn't allowing me to have a life of my own at all. Where all my friends were going out and having fun with friends, I had to go out and play the game. When I was old enough, I plucked up courage and told Dad that I didn't want to play any more as I had other things to do. He was really angry and disappointed in me, but I didn't care; I just didn't want to be trapped by this man into doing something I didn't want to do. That made him hate me more and become more aggressive towards me, so I was just living against the clock to become old enough to leave home. God, I couldn't wait.

I will never forget this, but someone I know was in hospital, having her first baby and her hubby called into see us. He said to me, 'Let's go out and have a drink to wet the baby's head.' I thought that was a good idea. But we set off in the car, and we were not going to a pub. We were heading down this country lane. He stopped the car and tried to get my clothes off and said, 'I have always fancied you, and if I had not married her, I would have asked you..' I was horrified as I had given him no come-on or anything. I got out the car and ran home alone. I told my mum, and she made me swear to keep it a secret and never to tell anyone, which I did till this day. But after that, I always kept my distance, and my mum made sure we were kept apart.

I will also never forget that when I started my period, my mum would not buy me pads or anything. So it was very embarrassing. What I did to survive was, I just folded up toilet paper on top of each other so it would leave me protected. Then my mum told me off for being extravagant with the toilet paper, but that was all I could do to protect myself. Also another thing that will stay with me forever, was that my mum would never buy me a toothbrush or toothpaste, and I didn't know any different as I didn't know that's what you had to do. But very embarrassingly, one Xmas, one of my friends bought me a toothbrush and toothpaste, as she was fed up with my bad breath. I was mortified and appalled that my mum had not accommodated me like a proper mother, but after that, I always made sure

I was very clean all the time. How could my mum not look after me and care for me like other mothers did?

Anyway life kept moving on. We did all the things that children do, and I finally became sixteen and started my first job, which was working in a supermarket. It was nice to have my own money and a little bit of independence. I met this really nice man, who was unhappy too as his mother had died and his dad had got remarried, and he did not get on at all with his stepmum. We became close as we both had our own problems at home. Hurriedly we found a flat and moved in together, and, before I knew it, we were married. He was a lovely man, soft and gentle, but was shy, so he could not show his true feelings. His job was a long distance lorry driver so was away from home most weeks. We had a nice home, but I was very alone and without love, and after a couple of years, I realised that we had got married for the wrong reasons. I wanted to do more than to be like a widow, home alone. All my friends around me were having babies and enjoying married life the proper way, spending time together, going out for walks, and doing the gardening together on a summer evening. Whereas for me, I would go home to an empty house and be on my own in the evenings. I only saw him at the weekends if I was lucky, and he would have to spend most of his time getting ready for the next week. I shocked everyone with my decision; it took me a lot of courage to finally say how I felt, but I thought I had to as otherwise my life would be a lie, as he was a very nice man. My parents hated me for deciding this as they really loved him; so did I, but not in the close way. Although we got divorced etc., we have always remained very close and the best of friends and were there for each other if needed. That bond will never go, which is good.

I went off and had a bit of fun and a bit of a life with the odd boyfriend, but nothing was right so just muddled on through life the best way I could. To be honest, because we didn't have the normal loving family, I didn't know what the proper way was. I was looking for something I didn't know.

Over the years, my first husband had moved away a good four hours' drive away, and I was in a situation I was not happy with. I seemed to keep making the same mistake over and over again, looking for something that I didn't know or understand. Then one morning, I had a call to tell me that my first husband had had a horrific road accident; he was critical and was fighting for his life. I was shocked and horrified and desperate to see him, so I rushed to go and see him. I saw him. He was in intensive care with all these tubes coming out of him, keeping him alive. 'Oh my god!' I couldn't believe that! My tummy was twisted, and I was so sad. How could this happen to him as he was such a good driver and such a good person? And this would have been the last person in the world I would have thought to have an accident.

I knew this was going to be a long time for recovery as he had terrible injuries, but I was sure that with the right love and help, he would recover. And I was going to dedicate myself to him to make sure that happened..

I visited him every day as he gradually got better. I will always remember that he had had a serious head injury and his hair was still full of dried blood. I asked the nurses if I could wash his hair. They said yes. So it was nice to fuss over him and make him look more like normal. He felt *so* much better. He had lost his voice due to a tracheotomy, so he had to have a lot of intensive therapy, which took a long time. Finally the day came when they said he could go home, so I obviously packed everything up and went home with him to look after him. We were so excited to be finally out of hospital and that he would be able to recover at home. I put a mattress on the floor beside his bed so that I could be there if ever he needed me, and over a long period of time, we got him back to 90 per cent health. That was a good time really; it gave him time to recover and gave me time to reflect on my life, and I thought to get my life back on track.

There was no way for us to be together again as we had more of a deep friendship than anything. I became restless and wanted love and a relationship, so I went through a paper to a dating agency. Finally this was where I met my second husband.

CHAPTER 2

After a few really nice phone calls that went very well, we decided to meet up on our first date. Obviously, it was nerve-racking, meeting for the first time. But we met and went out for a drink; we got on very well. He was good-looking, funny, charming, and very affectionate. *Bingo*! I thought, 'This is it! I have found him!' The date went so well, much better than I had expected. We arranged to meet up again and had lots more phone calls. He invited me to his house as he had a son, and he wanted me to meet him, which I did and we all got on very well. Well, I know now that he sucked, fooled, and wooed, me in really good, and I fell for his charm and his lies and before I knew it, I was in a dictatorship relationship. A couple of people had warned me to stay away as he was no good, but he was so nice that I could see no further than the trees. Before I knew it, I had moved in with him and was in a full-blown relationship, running around to his every need, doing everything he told me to do, and being completely subservient. How could I be so stupid? Although people had warned me, I thought it was because they were jealous and were just being malicious. So I ignorantly ignored everyone. I thought I was the luckiest woman in the world and he really loves me. God, I couldn't have been so wrong! What a fool!

I must say that the courting time was the best I had ever experienced, and I was completely smitten and thought life is finally good. I couldn't see the warning signs then—how he was getting stoned all the time. He tried to encourage me to try; he forced me to have sex, tried and insisted that we have sex with a third party and got me drunk. I had friends and every time they came to the house, he would make a move on them, but he was so funny that you couldn't help but like him and go along with it. He was definitely in control, and I was silly enough to let it happen. Behind the scenes, I couldn't see how I was fussing after him and looking after him like a mother. I never saw no wrong in that. I was so silly, and I realise now that I was so scared that I was too scared to do anything about it. I will never forget this; I know this was disgusting and I was stupid to let it happen, but I was too scared to say *no*. We would be driving along in the car—he would always drive—and he would take down his zip and order me to give him a blow job and would force me to continue till he had relieved himself. Or he would demand that I gave him a hand job, and I would have to do that for the continuation of the journey. I remember I would hate it, my arms and hands would ache and hurt, but I dare not stop, for the fear of being told off and threatened.

Within two years, I was pregnant and we were on our way to get married. He didn't want no family around, so it was a very private affair. He didn't get on well with his family at all. He was always falling out with them, especially his mum. So we flew off to Jamaica and had a lovely romantic wedding. I really thought my heart was complete.

I found it very hard as when you come from the United Kingdom, in different counties, you all have different accents, and mine was very different from his. So I couldn't help the way I spoke, but what started to frighten me was that if my accent popped out or I spoke a few of my local words, he would fly at me, tell me off, and tell me to speak properly. It got so bad that in the end I really had to think before I spoke and be careful that I didn't let my accent pop out for the fear of him going mad.

During the pregnancy, my alarm bells were ringing. He started to get stroppy and lose his temper more often, and he started talking to me as though I was something on his shoe. One day we had such a big row; he said, 'You are not going anywhere!' So he went and ripped the spark plug leads out of my car. I started to have these awful nosebleeds. On the odd occasion, I would sleep on the floor as I didn't want to be with him. He started becoming demanding. He would have a lie-in on Sundays, and I was to make no noise. If I did, he would go mad. So I would tiptoe round the house so as not to upset him, but I just put it down to the stress of a baby coming. My head was telling me to go, but I was just too scared to do anything as I knew he would come after me or never leave me alone if I did and I knew I couldn't handle it. I was trapped and foolishly believed that things would go back to normal once the baby was born.

As I said, he already had a son, and he had the social services involved with him when I met him. He told me that it was his ex-partner and how she had set him up and done all these nasty things. He was such a good liar and was so convincing that I actually felt sorry for him and thought there was no way this funny man would hurt anyone, especially his children. I was so sad to see that due to violence and abuse to his first girl friend, he was not allowed (as by the family court) to carry out the duties of a full time father. After blood tests etc.., it came up that the baby could be having Down's syndrome, so we had to go to a special hospital for scans and tests. They gave me 98 per cent confirmation that the baby was normal, so that was a relief for me.

Anyway, the baby was finally born, and it was like it happened overnight. He was a changed person. He became nasty, bossy, possessive, aggressive, and moody. He rejected the baby and started to get stoned more and life for me started to become a real hard chore. And the night the baby was born, my life changed, and this was the start of the end and also a start of a terrible, horrific journey.

Every day he had to wake up with a cup of tea in bed and all fresh, clean, pressed clothes waiting for him at the bottom of the bed. I would have to have his flask filled with hot tea and a packed lunch already in his bag. I had to fill up his tobacco tin and polish his boots that would be waiting for him by the door to ensure that he had a nice easy start to the day. In the winter, if it was cold, I had to warm up the bathroom for him before he got up, go out to defrost his van, and start the engine to warm up his van before he left. This carried on for ten years. I dared not, not do it as I would have to suffer the consequences. And it was so much easier to do it for a quiet life. I felt a prisoner in my own home.

Obviously by this time, I had a baby whom I loved so much and who meant the world to me. My dream was shattered as I had thought he was such a good dad; now that we had a baby of our own, he did nothing for it. He actually rejected her as he didn't want girls.

I had to look after not only him but a baby also as he did nothing. I remember when we were asleep and the baby woke up and started crying, he would angrily wake up, kick me in the bottom of the spine and say, 'Go and shut that fuckin' baby up.' So I often ended up sleeping on the floor besides the cot, so if the baby woke up again it would not disturb him. I was quite a strong person, so I managed and coped quite well. As he was not allowed to be near his previous partner, I did all the running around with his son also. If he needed anything for the house or building materials etc., I always had to go and get it for him and do all the running around for that, and as he would not look after the baby for me, I always had to take it with me. Also, if I was honest, I did not trust him either. I also had a full-time job, so I had the baby into childminding. It was also expected that the house be cleaned every day and kept immaculate. I was so upset that he had rejected the baby that his social worker became my friend, and she helped me to come to terms with that. I felt so empty, alone, and sad, and I thought, 'God, life is so hard and unfair. Why have I let this happen?' He also has a lovely baby. How could he reject her? That hurt so much. I was deeply saddened. He had turned into a different person, the complete opposite of the one whom I had married.

As the baby grew up a bit, he did play with it sometimes, but only on his terms and when it suited him. I suppose I managed to deal with it, and because of that, life was not too bad. We had our good times. His mum would visit sometimes, and he was horrid to her. He would often throw her out or tell her to fuck off out of his house and not to darken his door again. This was all in front of the baby. She would often come and see me when she knew he was not there. So we never had that bond with grandparents and siblings. I used to see my family sometimes as they lived four hours' drive away. My first husband used to take us, as his family lived near mine too, and it was nice to get away. As he was not family orientated, he never came with us. After three years, the inevitable happened. I became pregnant for the second time. I was very apprehensive and concerned but also happy that I had another baby on the way, as I loved being mum and loved my children very much. He was OK about it, but he did say, 'I hope it is a boy this time.'

I went ahead and continued what I always did. I also had the same test with this one, and it came out that it could be having Down's syndrome. So we had to go off and have the same tests and scans done. The results came out the same as before, so I was relieved to think that it was going to be normal.

The day came, and I went into hospital. I was quite worried, though, for my first child, as he was not good with looking after children and also she did not like him and was scared of him. And he was so pig-headed that he would not allow anyone to have her and look after (even her grandmother), but I thought, 'For the second child, you are out the next day, so that won't be too bad. She could manage OK for one night, then I would be home again.' No one had any idea of what he was like and how tense things were at home. We had all learnt to keep our life a secret; even my first child knew at that early age not to tell anyone. I was really anxious when I went into hospital, but I kept telling myself I can do this and it's only for one night.

Unfortunately it turned out the baby was breech, so I had to have an emergency Caesarean section, which went OK, but obviously I would have been better without.

The first night I was in hospital, he had a big row with his mum and fell out with all of his family. The next morning the doctors were doing their examinations and checks on everyone. My bed had the curtain around it as I was being examined, and I could hear someone crying outside. When the doctors left, I found his sister standing there, crying and begging me to have a word with him to calm down and apologise to everyone. It annoyed me a bit as I had just had a baby and was having all this hassle. Shortly after that, he turned up with my first child, moaning and complaining about having to stay home and look after our child etc. and that she was not eating. She was very upset to be with him and wanted to be with me. I took her down to the hospital canteen to see if I could get her to eat, but she was too upset, which worried me immensely. Anyway, this carried on for three days; I was beside myself. I was obviously really worried about our first child. I was not feeling too well myself, and I was being hounded by him to get out, and his family was hassling me to make things better. I couldn't believe it! I felt sick in my stomach. On the third day, he came in and was very angry and said, 'I want you home today as I have had enough of looking after this kid. That's your job.'

So I knew I had to do something fast and get out of there for the safety of my child. 'God!' I cried. 'Life is not fair. This is not fair.' I lied to the doctors and told them that my child was not eating and I was worried. First he said, '*No!* As you have had a Caesarean and you have to be in hospital for a minimum of five days at least.' He said that I could go home if I had someone to look after me. So I lied to him telling him that I had my mum with me and she was going to be there to help. So he reluctantly said yes. I knew this was not good for me. But I had no other choice. I had to go home.

So I hurriedly packed up all my stuff and the baby, and he took us home. My first child was so happy to see me going home; I had to do it for her. As soon as we got home, he said, 'Right! This is your job. I have had enough of babysitting. So I am off..'

He left, and I felt really overwhelmed and unwell and collapsed on the floor. I knew I could not do this on my own for a while, so I rang up my friend at the time and told her of the situation and asked her if I paid her would she help me for a couple of weeks, till I was back on my feet. I couldn't believe this! Here I was at home with a toddler and a newborn, with no family around me, especially their dad. I cried so much as I felt isolated and desperate.

She said yes and was there immediately. She was brilliant; she helped look after me and my eldest and keep the house tidy etc. He did not like my friend and made that more than obvious to her when he was there. He was very rude to her and nasty; it was very embarrassing. She hated him too, but she did not care. She was a very loyal friend. She knew I needed her help and couldn't do without her, so she just ignored him, which pissed him off immensely. Anyway, on the third day of us being out of hospital, he went mad and lost his temper big time. Whilst we were sitting in the lounge feeding the baby and my eldest was playing, he called each member of his family one by one, told them what he thought of them told them to fuck off and that he never liked them and never wanted to see them again and that they were banned from coming to our house and we were to have nothing to do with them. When he got off the phone, he instructed me that I was banned from seeing them and they were not allowed to come into the house. And that they were not allowed to see our children. That was very upsetting and made me feel very awkward as I didn't have a problem with his family. Plus it was the children's grandparents and family. I was so distraught. At this time, my eldest was three, and she was upset and asked him, 'Why can't I see nanny and Granddad?'

He shouted at her and told her to shut the fuck up. It was really hard having to explain this to a three-year–old. It broke my heart and I felt so bad, but in her own way, she seemed to understand and so she never mentioned it to him again and got on with life as it was. So if I saw them in the town, I had to ignore them and look the other way and keep my head down, which was awful. I hated it. I used to come over all panicky, anxious, and hot as I hated it. So because I found this hard and did not want to put my children through any difficult times, I used to shop out of town so that it would be very unlikely that we would bump into anyone. I was so scared. I wondered, 'Who can I talk to? Who can I tell? Who can help us?' I felt so desperate. Why has life got to be so cruel?

A week after this, I went down to spend a few days with my family. I broke down in front of them and told them what had happened. My parents hated him and hated us being with him, but they knew there was nothing they could do as they knew how frightened of him we were. My parents seemed to have mellowed in their older age and were nicer and more supportive now that all us kids had grown up. They comforted us and helped us to gain courage to go back and carry on with life. My God! Life couldn't get much worse surely. They didn't want us to go back, but they knew I had to.

The new baby seemed to be getting ill a lot and having chest infections, so I was backwards and forward to the doctors and she had all these medicines. They eventually diagnosed her with asthma. This made me so angry, hurt, and frustrated as there would be our new baby lying in her cradle and there he would be sitting smoking a joint, and it would be like the room was full of smog. The ignorant pig didn't care. And I dared not tell him to stop as I knew what he would do and say.

By this time, the nice side of him had completely vanished. He was very angry, abusive, and dominating. He didn't help me at all with the children, and at night, if one used to cry, he would still always kick me out of bed and tell me to shut them up. So I suppose I went into overdrive, thinking, 'I have two children whom I love very much and want them to have a life as good as possible.' So I ran around, making sure that he was well catered for in everything and that the children were OK and enjoying life the best way I could. They had both realised that he was aggressive and shouted a lot, so they were very scared of him. They were very timid and didn't want to be with him at all. I used to take them swimming, to playschool, etc. He didn't care where I went with them as long as they were not with him. God, I felt so sad and desperate. How could this be happening? My poor girls! They were lovely, and their father was a complete moron and was such a let-down to them. What also made me cross was that he was so false in front of people. I so wanted to tell people the truth but couldn't. I was so trapped.

I also remember one day—I used to work for this multimillionaire. Not only did I clean her mansion, but she held dinner parties, and when she did, she asked me and a few others to be the waitresses and look after the guests. This was great and, say, once a year we did this. The last time, I was going to have to work on a Sunday. He was annoyed with me as he would be left with the girls. I was rushing around in the kitchen, getting meals ready for them, whilst he was sitting at the breakfast bar, holding my youngest as she was still a baby. He was getting stoned, and I was getting concerned. He just dropped her on the stone floor, banging her head. *God*! I ran and picked her up and called him a bastard and said he had done that on purpose to stop me from going. She was crying, and her head was red. I couldn't take any chances as she could have damaged herself, so I immediately called and said I could not work that day. We spent the rest of the day in the hospital, scanning and observing her. I just could not believe how he could have done that as you don't just drop a baby and hurt your child. Well, he got his wish that day. I didn't go to work and he didn't have to look after the girls, but, man, what a price to pay.

I often went to see my parents with the kids and leave him at home, as he was not family orientated. We often argued; his favourite sayings were 'A woman should be seen and not heard' and 'You do as I say, not do as I do'. He often forced me to have sex against my will and told me that I had to carry out my marital duties. I used to lie there in the dark, crying quietly with my head in the pillow. No one had any idea what this monster was doing, and I was too scared to tell anyone. He often used to have me pinned up against the wall, shouting as loudly as he could, or he would throw things at me. I remember one time I was in the bath. He burst in with an electric toaster plugged in, threatening to electrocute me. Fortunately, he put it down. He would give me jobs and orders to do every day. I had to do them, or he would be so angry when we got home. I had to have the girls' toys packed away and the rooms tidy. He would phone me to check where I was and what I was doing, and if I was with a friend, he would go mad and tell me, 'That's not what I told you to do today.' So I had to make excuses and get home as soon as I could. I was so trapped, terrified, and isolated. I honestly used to cry and think that I could not do this any more. What was I going to do? I was becoming a nervous wreck. By this time, he was smoking more weed, but I thought it was more important for us to try and keep a family together. So we talked about immigrating for a fresh start and better future for the children. We made enquires and did all the legal things that had to be done and were soon accepted in New Zealand. I really believed that this would be good for us—get away from all the old crap, move on, and start a fresh. I thought we may have a chance. How stupid was I? There was I, thinking I could change a man that was who he was and set in his ways. I was constantly living in fear and anxiety; it was not good. I needed help. But I was too scared to ask or tell anyone. The feeling of isolation was immense. I thought, 'Please, let someone help me, but where the hell do I start? And if I did he will turn against me.' I knew he would hunt me down and not leave us alone. My life was horrid, and I thought I had no way out.

So we hurried round and sold everything and packed up all that we wanted to bring with us. I must say I was scared to death, but I had a voice saying to me, 'You have to try.' Not long before we left, I remember we had a big row. He told me to fuck off, and he would go to New Zealand on his own and leave us here. I said that he was not going on his own; these were his kids and we had a responsibility to keep us all together. He never replied to that, so we just muddled on through packing. We sold our house, so we had to live in his friend's house. We also had a lovely little Lhasa apso dog, which we had cleared and were going to take with us. Also, the girls loved it very much, but sadly, one day he ran out of the drive and got killed instantly, which was devastating. It broke our hearts as we loved him heaps. So we sadly had to bury him in the garden and leave him behind. He got fed up with the friend whose house we were staying in, and he abused the crap out of her one night and said, 'Right! We are leaving. We have to find somewhere else to live.'

I couldn't believe it, as though it was not stressful enough as it was. Fortunately we found somewhere else to live for a couple more months. We said our goodbyes, which was rather upsetting and much harder than I had thought; it was so sad. We had to go down and see my family to say goodbye. I will never forget that as that was the first time I ever saw my dad cry. He broke down as I went to give him an embracing hug, and that choked me up. I felt sick. Was this my dad? The man that was such a bastard when I was young. As usual, my mum was emotionless, which was nothing unusual. I must say that that was one of the hardest things I have ever had to do. Also I didn't realise how many nice friends I had till I left; I did feel very scared and concerned, saying, '*God*! What am I doing? Is this the right thing to do? Should I be leaving all these lovely people?' Everyone was really sad to see me go, but I thought I had to do this for the sake of my children. I was sure that by moving away from all the old habits, things would settle down and get better. Just before we left, he received a package from his mum with all our photos ripped in half even the children's, saying, 'I am glad you are moving away, and I will never have to see you again..' He laughed it off, which was disgusting, but there was no way you could convince him to change his mind or see it any other way. And there was no way you could get him to make peace before he left, which I thought was very important. He was so pig-headed and headstrong.

There were quite a few people concerned for us as by this time, some people had an inkling of what he was like. But I still had said nothing to anyone, apart from a very dear person whom I had worked with for three years, and he had become like my adopted dad. Before I left, he pulled me aside and said, 'I am worried for you, and just in case anything goes wrong over there and you need to come home in an emergency, well then I want you to know that all you do is call me and I will fly you back from New Zealand urgently.' I cried and gave him a big hug; I couldn't believe that he would do that for me, and I always have and always will love him very much. Although he was much older than me, he has always been really kind to me and was always there for me if I needed him.

So after we had said all our goodbyes and got all our belongings in a container on a ship, we were on the way to New Zealand. It was time to set off on our journey..

So we set upon our journey to New Zealand.

CHAPTER 3

We finally arrived in New Zealand. In January 2003, the children were six and three. As we arrived in summer, everything looked nice and hot. We stayed with my cousins for a while, as we had nowhere to live and to give us a chance to find a home. He found a job immediately as he was a tradesman, and they were in short supply. We looked hard for a house, but it was difficult as houses were so different from what I was used to. We did not like them much, and in the end, he lost his temper once again and told me that I had to buy this fuckin' house 'cause he wasn't looking at any more and we had to like it. This was just in time as all our furniture had arrived on the ship. I felt very sad as stupidly my first dream had been knocked. I thought that this was a fresh start for us, and I couldn't choose the house to live in.

I must say it was very hard at first not knowing anyone; everything was so different and hard to get used to. The children settled into kindy and school really well; he could not settle in a job. He would often fall out with someone and have to look for another job. As things were different for him he would loose his temper or come home frustrated as work wasn't going how he expected to. He also got stopped for speeding lots of times the first couple of months we were here, and you could tell he was angry when you heard him do a wheelspin down the drive and a screech of his brakes; we would all look at one another and sigh, 'oh no, not again!' So we would quietly work around him for the fear of him getting worse. I worked part-time so that I always could be there for the children. For the first year it was hard, we had lots of visitors come to see us from UK, which was nice. It would be exciting going to the airport and getting friends and my mum and dad as they all wanted to see where we were living and how we had settled in, but it was very sad taking them back to the airport to go home. We gradually made new friends here, especially me from school, as everyone was so friendly. So although things were not perfect, I thought that if we tried, we could make this work. He worked hard and seemed to settle better in a job, and I just carried on with what I normally did and that was looking after the girls, home, my job and making sure that he was well looked after. I have to be honest. I hated my life; I totally regretted moving here as he made it so hard for me, but I worked hard for the sake of the girls and kept telling myself that I can do this.

But sad to say I was so wrong; things got from bad to worse. I thought to myself, 'What the hell have I done? I have made the biggest mistake of my life. How am I going to get out of this? Who can help us?' God, I felt so alone and desperate. As I had never had drugs before or been involved with drugs, I did not know that over here weed was in such big supply as people grew it all over the place. So he was taking a lot more than he used to take. He was getting very unpredictable and aggressive towards me and the children. It got so bad that we did not want to come home any more and dreaded the time we were there. Everyone walked on egg shells and went around the house as quietly as we could so we didn't make him angry. Weekends were awful; the rule was that he had to have a lie-in, and we dare not wake him up. Doing that with two small children was hard, so I used to get up and go for a walk or take them to the park or go swimming or something, so that he could be on his own and have his own space and quiet. The girls would plead with me, 'Mummy, let's leave him,' or say, 'Mummy, do we have to go home?' It used to break my heart, as I was not strong enough and I was failing them. It was tearing me apart. I felt so sick and desperate, and the isolation was immense.

He would never eat with us. If I had cooked him a meal previous, trying to save me from cooking later, he would throw it at me so I would either be wearing his dinner, or it would be running down the wall. It may be a nice roast dinner, and he would scream at me, 'I am not eating this fuckin' shit! Cook me something proper!' He would often have a drink, and he would lose his temper and throw it over me. So I would be left dripping in juice, water, or beer. He would throw his keys or anything he had in his hands at my face; he broke my tooth in on one attempt. This was done in front of the children, and by that time, they were very scared for their and my safety and would often shout and scream to him to stop. He would reply by shouting, 'Shut the fuck up.'

I was exhausted and desperate for my children, and I kept thinking, 'There must be something I can do as I cannot live like this. We can't carry on any more. I have to get help somewhere.'

As it was hot, the windows would be open. He would come home and go mad, stamping around the house, shouting, 'Shut these fuckin' windows! If they are open tomorrow when I come home from work, I will fuckin' glue them all together.' So after that, just before I knew he was due home, I would run around, making sure that all the windows were shut disregarding if it was hot or not. It was awful; my stomach churned all the time, not knowing how he would be when he got home or what he would say or do next. He was so cruel. He told me that I smelt and my breath was disgusting. He used to pull funny faces at me and go yuk! This gave me a real complex, and I still live with that now. I clean my teeth so many times a day, and I always talk to anyone with my hands in front of my mouth if I am close. If not, I talk facing sideways. I have been told I don't smell, but he did it so much that it has left me tormented by it.

By this time, my eldest was at the stage that she liked her music and she would often have it playing in her room; he would burst in there, shouting at her, threatening her that if she had it up loud again, he would cut the fuckin' plugs off. She then started to live like a hermit, creeping around the house, as we dared not be loud like normal people.

My youngest, she was at the stage where she played with her toys on the floor. He would shout walking through them, kicking them everywhere, hitting her with them in the process. She would cry, so she then used to play in her room and not play outside their from then on for the fear of him loosing his temper again. Once they had left their bikes out on the deck; he went crazy and grabbed hold of them, throwing them off the deck, shouting, 'If they are here again, I will fuckin' get my car and run over and flatten them.' It was a good job the girls were not under the deck as he would have hit them; he dented them up slightly by the force of them hitting the ground. The girls were screaming and crying; it was sheer hell, and we were in a desperate situation. 'What the hell can I do? Who can help us? I need help and am stuck and trapped. I have to do something for the sake of my girls..' I was crying from inside, as I was in sheer disbelief that this was happening.

They both had rabbits. He was cutting the grass one day, and he went mad, lost his temper, and turned the rabbit hutch upside down, hurting and frightening them. He actually killed them; the girls were so upset that they shouted at him, pleading with him to stop—which was awful, as he was shouting at the top of his voice, 'You should move these fuckin' rabbits, or I will wring their necks.' They were crying loudly. I could not believe I had allowed this to happen. I comforted them and distracted them to something else, and for the rest of that day, we just stayed out of his way. The girls hated him so much that they wouldn't interact with him and were scared to put a foot wrong.

As he was a tradesman, he came home with the idea one day that he was going to build a growing room under the house. He had the knowledge how to do it, and he would grow it under my youngest daughter's bedroom. We argued heaps, and I pleaded with him not to do it. He threw me across the room and told me to shut the fuck up and if I didn't like it I should fuck off. He was going to do it regardless, which scared me to death. I also remember the day when I accidently threw his lighter out in the bin; he went absolutely off his head. When he got home, he went out and tipped the wheelie bin upside down and went through the rubbish till he found it; then he made me tidy and clean it all up. And called me a dumb fuckin' thick bitch, and if I didn't do as I was told, he would put me in the bin. The girls started screaming again, and he then said, 'You can fuckin' shut them up as well.' He often used to shout to me 'a woman should be seen and not heard'. He used to spend a lot of the time in the garage, sometimes with his drug mates, drinking beer, and if he ran out, he would shout out to me, 'Oy! Go and get some more beer.' And because the children did not want to be with him, they came with me everywhere.

We had also got ourselves a new puppy, as ours had died before we left UK. The dog used to bark at him when he was going crazy, so he often kicked it in the stomach, making it fly across the front room. He would often get stoned and get the dog's mouth touching his and blow smoke in his mouth, in front of the children. They often cried. My eldest one night said to him, 'I wish you were dead and you were not my dad', as he had thrown a cigarette lighter at her face, hitting her eye.

He flew at me for that, shouting, 'Are you going to let her talk to me like that?' My youngest would not go near him, not even talk to him; they never wanted him to put them to bed or take them anywhere as they did not feel safe whatsoever.

I will never forget but most people would look forward and enjoy Xmas to be a nice family affair, but I used to dread Xmas as I had two excited girls that wanted to enjoy their presents etc. But we all had to wait for him to wake up and have a cup of tea and a joint before he was ready to open presents, and telling that to two excited girls who couldn't wait to open their presents was cruel and hard. But if we did not comply with his demands, it would develop into a big row and we didn't want that, especially on Xmas evening. So they had to just sit there and wait for him to do what he wanted before they could do anything.

Things just got worse. If ever I had a female friend round, he would always be suggestive to them or come on to them, which was very embarrassing. He started telling me that I smelt and my breath was really bad, so he gave me a complex. Still to this day, I will not talk up close to people, and I always hold my hand over my mouth if I am close to people, and I am constantly cleaning my teeth, although I am told I am OK.

He also always used to keep telling me I was fat, ugly, and thick as shit, which I still think to this day. And it has left me with little confidence and not a high opinion of myself.

So my day consisted of getting him up, making sure everything was OK for him to leave for work, then get the girls up, and get them ready for school. Go to work myself, clean the house, do the washing etc., get the girls, do their homework or things regarding school. Do dinner for us and for him and then go to bed absolutely exhausted. One day we had to go out for some reason, and he was his normal self. The girls were strapped in, in the back; he started shouting and arguing. I told him to take us home. He went mad, shouting, 'You wanna go home, ay? How about I kill you all right now?' With that, he speedily went round the roundabout, trying to tip the car and crash it. The girls were screaming and crying; it was awful. Fortunately he did not succeed. We went home, and he sped off. My God! That day was horrific! It haunts me; we were so lucky to be alive as he was so angry and so close to crashing the car. The girls would not go out with him after that. By then, anyway, we were living practically separate lives as I could not bear to be with him. I was so scared and anxious whenever we were around him. He would go out a lot now too, often take off in the evenings etc. I used to find that a relief as he was not home, upsetting the children. It was really getting to me now. I was scared to death, so were the girls. I was scared to tell anyone or do anything as I never knew what he would do, and he would never leave me alone. What the hell was I going to do?

In the last year of us being together, there was a huge decline in his mental well-being. It became quite scary. He collapsed one day in the kitchen. I called the ambulance; they found him to be very stoned, and dehydrated. This really upset the girls too. By this time, I was sleeping in the spare room, and it was a case of us and him, and everyone tiptoed round him. My eldest had become very friendly with some lovely people, and every weekend, she tried to go and stay with them. They took her to church every Sunday. He started to complain about that and banned her from going. He said she should be at home. He would never let them go out to play, and he would hardly talk to them. He used to say to me, 'That is a woman's job.' So there was quite a barrier between us. Things were really bad at home. We were desperately unhappy and scared but every day we would get up and get in the car and put our smiley faces on, so no one had any idea what was really going on. As I said, things had got really bad by this time, and I had collapsed. Then one day, I was taking the girls swimming. We were so upset and traumatised that when a boy ran in front of me, I started to feel funny all over and sick. We went over the barrier, and my eldest quickly stepped in and crashed my car into a tree to stop the car from rolling into the river. I had passed out, and I was advised to see my doctor from the ambulance which had been called out to check us up. After this, all he kept doing was call me mental and mentally deficient. I went and saw the doctor on the recommendation from the ambulance team. I explained our situation, and the doctor was quite horrified and concerned about our well-being and recommended that I go for counselling as I was in an emotional state. After I had gone to see her two times, and told her everything, she told me that it was very obvious that our marriage was over and that we were being badly abused and that I had to do something. Because I had been talking to her, I felt a bit more confident with the support she gave me. He said, 'I don't know who you are hanging around with, but you are talking too much and knowing too much and I am going to ban you from speaking with anyone.'

I was torn apart and really scared as the girls were asking me to leave, and I knew we could not carry on like this. But I knew what he was capable of, and I just didn't know what to do.

Anyway, on 26 July 2006, it was taken out of my hands. He came home from work, and you could tell he was in an aggressive mood. He was very nasty to me for no reason. He started to become argumentative, and my main concern was to keep my girls safe as this monster was capable of doing anything and I wasn't going to let that happen. He went crazy and snatched my purse out of my bag, took all my bank cards off me, cut them all up, and told me to fuck off, but if I left with the kids, he would kill us, or he would hunt us down wherever we were and kill us. He threatened to find us and set fire to our house, or if he saw me walking on the side of the road, he would mow me down from behind and kill me. My eldest daughter tried to phone the police, but he started raving and cut the phone cord. And I have to say that that threat is still very real to this day to all three of us. The girls were pulling him off me, begging him to leave me alone; they were so upset. It was terrible, a complete nightmare. Finally he got up, took his keys, and sped off. My God! At that time, I felt sick, numb, and horrified. I thought, 'What the hell am I going to do? How am I going to cope? How am I going to protect the children? We can't stay here any more. It's over, we have to move out. *Now*!'

With that, I called my best friend at the time, and I called my counsellor as she lived just up the road from me; all three of us were in a dreadful state, screaming, crying, and scared to death. I knew then that we had to leave as there was no way we were safe any more, and that was the end. My friend drove up and picked us up and took us to my counsellor. My eldest was in a state of shock and was wrapped in a blanket; the youngest couldn't stop crying, and she would not let go of me. My counsellor called the police as we were in a dreadful situation. Plus he had threatened to kill us. They came and took a statement and said they were going to arrest him. I advised them that he had gone out. They said, 'Don't worry. We will wait.' I also advised them that he was very aggressive and maybe two policemen would not be enough. They told me not to worry.

I was in a state of shock and terrified for our safety as he was a very dangerous man. We talked with the police, and I said that we had nowhere to go and we couldn't be where he knew where we were as he would kill us.

I explained that for our safety I wanted to go home back to UK as I knew we would be safe there, and I wouldn't feel safe anywhere in New Zealand. They advised me that he could have me charged for taking the children out of the country, but I said, 'That is the risk I am prepared to take.' I felt so desperate. At that time, I felt there was no other option, and any other caring mother in my situation would do the same thing.

I remembered what my dear friend had said to me before we left UK in the beginning that if there was anytime we had to come home in an emergency, then call him. So that night, I rang him and explained what had happened and said it was urgent that we left. Both girls were in a state and wanted to leave also, so he booked and paid for the tickets that same night. Later that night, I got a text from my husband saying where was I. He was waiting in the dark for me and was going to kill me. I was terrified. I felt sick in my gut and was so worried for my children's safety. I knew he would do it as he was so unstable.

The next morning, the police called me, saying that they had arrested him during the night and he was very angry and not happy at all and had been making his views known in the cells. And said that they were going to discharge him later that afternoon, so if I wanted to get to the house to collect anything it was best to go now as they could see how aggressive he was and they were concerned for our safety and welfare. So we went round to the house, got three suitcases, and filled them with as much clothes and personal items as we could and left. I really got on well with my neighbours and felt the need to explain and say goodbye. We went and knocked on the door, and when we told them, they were very sad and shocked and wished us well. We had a flight booked for the UK at 6.30 p.m. that night, and we were all terrified and I couldn't relax until I knew we were safe on that plane home. This was the only thing I could do for the safety of my children. And anyone else in my position would have done the same, with all their family back home. I could have had him charged with threatening to kill us, but my children's safety was so important to me that I didn't care if he got charged or not. Apparently, he was charged with that, but then the charges were dropped as we were not there. A silly mistake I made, but I did what I thought was best at the time. We nervously drove to the airport as I had no idea where he was, and whether he had thought that we might be on a plane, and if he would be at the airport, or he had put a ban on us leaving, or I would get arrested for kidnapping the children. So it was a very tense time, checking in. I was looking out for anyone trying to stop us; we finally got to the departure gate and said some emotional goodbyes. We got on the plane and sat in our seats. My eldest was crying and said, 'Mummy, we have done it. We are safe.' I quietly sighed a sigh of relief knowing that we were safe but not knowing what the future had for us. But I was also very sad with what had happened and that we had left everything behind and just come away with our clothes in a suitcase. I had to walk away from our marital home, leaving all our personalised items and sentimental items behind and just had to leave everything, not knowing if we would ever see that again. The girls had left all their toys behind, but they did not care. They were happy and more relieved that we had finally done it and run away from the worst situation ever. I was emotionally and psychologically exhausted and the girls were too, and we huddled together on the plane. Both girls fell asleep with their heads on my lap; we could finally sleep knowing we could be safe. But—this is a big but—I was terrified of what lay ahead of us.

You know what was the biggest shock of them all? After two days of us leaving our marital home, he was seeing someone else, and after three days of our departure, she moved into our home. But obviously, you would not get the truth from them as they would conspire together. I was shocked and in true disbelief and wondered if this had been a plot that he had planned to happen a long time ago. Which devastated me as I had no idea; that hadn't even crossed my mind. How could he treat me and our daughters like shit, smoke drugs, and have an affair? What a moron!

After a long flight home, we finally touched down in London. We had our friends waiting for us. It was very emotional reunion, but I was glad to go home. We were really tired and still in a state of shock, but we were so relieved to be home on safe ground with no death threat. Everyone was so happy to see us safe and sound. It did not take us long to get settled into life in UK as people were so kind and helpful and understanding, but I must say that we missed New Zealand. My eldest started a new school, which she liked. Then I thought I had better write him a letter. I explained to him what we had done and why. Not long after that, I got an order summoning me to court through the Hague Convention, ordering us to go back to New Zealand. I was gutted and in a state of shock as I really did not think he would want to put us through all of that, but I guess I underestimated the depths of his nasty behaviour. I quickly got a good barrister and thought we had enough evidence on us to allow us to stay, as we all felt safer and happier. Unfortunately, we did not succeed, which I guess in the back of my mind I had thought we wouldn't as I knew what he was capable of, how forceful and vindictive he could be. Plus he had to be in control and had no empathy for what he did to anyone else but himself. Although, the judge said, 'I can see why you are here, and I think it's in your best interest to stay here, but sadly I have to send you back due to the Hague Convention, and you have to fight it there. But I do realise you have a dangerous husband, and I will send you over with an order making you safe on your arrival.'

Everyone was very sad and disappointed that we had to go back, but that was the law. He paid for the flights home, so our journey was all booked and we left UK. It was soul-destroying and worrying what lay ahead for us as I knew it would not be easy. Also, whilst we were in UK, he had managed to threaten and intimidate my good friends and family, which put us in a very precarious situation. It became obvious to me that he would harass, bully, or threaten anyone that was going against him. I don't know exactly why I never had the courage to leave him before as I knew how he worked and what he was capable of. Also, my old neighbours contacted me and said how he was abusing, intimidating, and bullying them and being awful. So much so, she sent her husband away as he is a lovely old quiet man and couldn't put up with the terrible behaviour. I spoke with her, and in my defence, she offered to write an affidavit to the court telling them what he was doing. He obviously found out about that, and he would wake them up at like 2 a.m., shouting abuse at them in the driveway, calling them terrible names, and pulling his pants down and showing his bottom to them. It was horrible, and I felt so embarrassed of him. The bad thing was that they obviously tried to report it to the police, but because his girlfriend had moved into our home, she just stood by him, lying and denying it. So there was nothing the police could do.

As I knew this was going to be a hard battle and how good he was at lying, I needed witnesses to prove that he was hostile and violent. So I got old evidence out about him from the past. Plus I contacted old employees, and they all had their own story to tell. And yes, you guessed it, after that, he bullied them all also. I thought to myself, 'There is no end to this. Am I going to cope? I am not going to be able to win against such a powerful man.'

Another long flight back and we finally arrived back In Auckland. I had no idea what lay ahead. We had nothing, and I knew what he was capable of doing and so did the girls. So we were all very reluctant and anxious. We were really nervous when we arrived at the airport as I imagined he would be there somewhere. As he had booked the flights, so he knew all our details. Fortunately we did not see him, but he would have been there somewhere.

We had nowhere to stay, so we lived with my friend for a while. I appointed a barrister immediately. We went ahead and sold the marital home and were separated. I lost most of my personal possessions and belongings, and the girls lost most of their favourite toys. He did give them some things, but they stunk of cigarette smoke and the girls just did not want them. So we threw most of it away.

Here started a long, strenuous five-year court battle.

CHAPTER 4

As I said at first, I did the first thing that had to be done and that was to sell the marital home, which was very unfair as he had lied and made a lot of false accusations. He also kept a lot of things that were mine. I couldn't be bothered to fight it out with him; all I wanted was a peaceful life and to be left alone. This was my chance now to move on with our lives and get away from the demonstrative behaviour from a husband and a father. Not only that, I had realised that nothing would be fair as far as he was concerned as he didn't know the word 'fair'. It had to be his way or not at all. So I knew it was going to be a hard, scary battle.

But I have to say that there is a load of women out there who are in the same situation and cannot see no end to a dreadful, abusive situation. But remember, you can do anything if you put your mind to it, and there is light at the end of the tunnel. You have to fight for what you believe in. The hardest thing of all is getting the courage to face up to the fear and break that cycle, but once you have done that and got support from the right authorities, it is much easier, believe me. And that is why I want to give ladies the confidence and the courage to break that cycle as it is so important and there is no looking back after that. And you would never regret it.

Once everything had been agreed by the lawyers, the house was sold. By this time, the girls had gone back to the school they were at before we left and had settled in quite well. I was always on tenterhooks as I never knew when he would turn up or what he would do as I knew he was capable of anything. But I tried hard to be as calm as possible for the sake of the girls, and I did not want to worry them. I was also concerned that he was capable of making up false allegations and accusations, and I never knew what was going to turn up at my door. Also, I didn't know if the girls could be safe at school without him turning up at anytime, as once he had made his mind up about anything he would do it regardless.

The most annoying thing was he would gladly just deny anything he said or did, regardless of what effect it had on the girls, but for some things, there were proofs and evidence and he couldn't really deny them, but he did so with full support of his girlfriend.

After that, he put his claim in that he wanted custody of the children and that I was an incapable mother and I was mentally ill, so unsuitable to look after his children. I knew this could not happen as that was not what they wanted and it would be very damaging to them if it did, as it was all lies, unfair, very hurtful, and dirty. So I appointed a good barrister. She recommended that the first thing we do was to go to court and get a protection order to make us safe. God, I hated this monster. He made my tummy feel sick at all times. Living in fear was awful, and it was terrible for the children to be living on their nerves. I hated this man so much for what he was doing, and he had no empathy whatsoever. Because of his aggressive and abusive behaviour, it was not long before the judges saw his true colours, and for that, we were awarded the protection order as there were concerns for our safety and sanity. I was also destroyed as he managed to convince the judge that I had kidnapped his children as I had been planning to run away to the UK for months and that was all to do with my plan and I lied about his threats to kill, etc. It was so painful having to sit there and listen to this crap. As I said, he would do or say anything to get what he wanted. I know I did the wrong thing going to UK, but I did what I thought was best for my children at the time, which I see now was the wrong thing. But once you are in a situation that I was in, any caring mother would have done the same. Anyway, he convinced the judge that I was a threat and would do it again, so he put an order on the children against removing them from New Zealand so that we could not leave the country. Which, I have to say, frustrated me as I had no intention of doing it again; I was desperate.

We had to go to court, which, I must say, was gut-wrenching and nerve–racking. The girls also had to go and see barristers on a regular occurrence due to his lies and false allegations. They also had to see child psychologists and go over it again and again, which broke my heart as it was so destroying to them. It was unfair, seeing them have to go through all of this and not being able to protect them. Gladly, we had the protection order, which made us reasonably safe, but it still did not give us 100 per cent guarantee. And he was insistent that he was right and I was wrong and kept lying and making up stories about me and the girls. And there seemed to be no limit this man would not hesitate in going to. The judge did see sense though. Not only did he reward us a protection order, but he also gave me day-to-day care of the children, which was a huge relief. But I knew he was not going to stop there. This was disgusting. He was meant to be a caring father, and here he was lying to get his own way, regardless of any cost to his children.

The pressure was so great and the fear was so intense that it was hard to get up every day, not knowing how we were going to cope. By this time, my eldest was very unhappy and asking to die. She was also so aggressive. My youngest, practically overnight, broke out in all these warts all over her hands, fingers, feet, and knees. It was horrid, so I took her immediately to see the doctor. He said it was nothing to worry about. I forgot the legal name, but he said they were stress warts and when everything calmed down they would go as fast as they came. Which they did. It was very ironic 'cause he kept harassing my barrister, accusing me of not caring for his child enough and that I had to take her to get it sorted. But after she told him that he had to pay to see a specialist, he shut up. I remember we went shopping one day. The girls wanted something particular, so I sent them off to the supermarket to get it. Whilst they were away, I came across very ill and feeling very unwell, I collapsed on the floor. By the time the girls came back to me, I was surrounded by well-wishers, and an ambulance had been called. Obviously the girls were very upset and worried. We all went to hospital in the ambulance. The girls called my best friend, who, I must say, has been a godsend to me and without her today I would not be here. She has been with me through thick and thin, seen me at my worst and my best, and also came to every appointment that I have had. She has been a godsend to me, and I will always be eternally grateful to her. As soon as they called her, she came to the hospital, and she took us home and cared for us. She is my best friend and has become like my sister. We are very close, and I love her heaps and always will. Due to the hospital instructions, I went to see my new doctor, because as we were starting out afresh, I needed to register with everything oblivious to him as I did not want him anywhere near us or cause us any harm. My doctor said that

I was under extreme stress and trauma and I needed medication to help me deal with the situation, and, I must say, I have the same doctor today. He has been marvellous and helped me through all of this activity and I wouldn't be here without him either. He has been a tower of strength to me. He was like a normal doctor. He understood what the three of us had gone through, and he has been there for us every step of the way. He took the time to listen to us and help us the best way he could and supported us all the way. I must say that without him, I would not be here; he is the best doctor I have ever had, and I cannot thank my best mate and doctor enough. I am sure I must have got on my doctor's nerves, as I have been in there heaps with all sorts of conditions and complaints and he helped me through everyone of them. For that I am entirely grateful.

Knowing I was under supreme stress and anxiety, people were trying to help us all they could. The next trauma was that he applied for visitation rights, which I knew was going to be hard as there was no way he was going to give up and there was no way they wanted to see him. After a few really strenuous court battles, listening to his lies and false allegations, even the judge got frustrated with him and said, 'You are throwing false allegations and accusations around like confetti.' If anyone went against his expectations or against him, they would be on his hit list; we had to sit in a private room as he would get threatening to me in the corridor, and as soon as I walked into the courtroom, he would be very intimidating. If we walked into the corridor, we could hear him shouting already. Once we were in court, he would start shouting, and the judge had to keep warning him. Once, he said, 'This is fuckin' bullocks', threw his file across the room, and walked off and told the judge to fuck himself. The endless complaints he put in against the judges and barristers were unreal. After a load of false codswallop, unbelievably, he was awarded supervised access! I will never forget when I went home and told them that they had to see him every other weekend, they were gutted and so upset. It was awful having to take them to the centre, knowing I had to drop them off, making them see him. I was crushed and gutted; I felt sick and frustrated as there was nothing I could do to protect my children. What a shit mother I was, allowing my children to go through all this crap. And what the hell! What was the justice system thinking of? But the truth of the matter was that he had done what I had feared. He had managed to fool people and convince them around to his way of thinking. By bullying and lying, he even accused me of having an affair, of being gay and bisexual. There was no limit to this monster.

Some of the visits were so bad; he would try his hardest to bribe, threaten, or blackmail them to do things they didn't want to do, and they would be in a terrible state when I picked them up. That was terribly distressing to me to see my girls suffering the way they were. If I tried to report what he had done, he would deny it, or he would have been cleverly doing his mind games on my girls to save himself, which was soul-destroying to them. It was like taking them to the torture chamber. I felt sick every other Saturday when I had to take them; they didn't sleep very well the night before either. I thought, 'What the hell am I going to do? I have got a monster here. He has deceived everyone. How can this be? And there is nothing I can do.'

It was terrible. The morning they had visits, they would be crying on the way, 'Mummy, I don't want to go. Don't take us. We don't want to see him.' Once I picked them up, they would be angry. My eldest would destroy anything she had made with him; she would stamp on it or break it, crying angrily, 'Mummy, I hate this. I don't want to come here.' My youngest would just cry and say nothing. He would then start pushing for more and expect more. I remember one of the things that really upset them was that he used to take his partner to the visits, and she would try and push her way into the equation. What would upset the girls immensely was that she would wear my clothes that I had left behind. They were very upset by this when I picked them up. He was so cunning and false that he would trick the supervisors to go out for two seconds, enough to say, 'I know where your mum lives. I know what car she drives.' And he would be flicking a penknife on his key ring. The girls would be so scared after their visits. One weekend, my eldest was so convinced that he knew where we lived and knew what car we had that we had to change everything around with my best friend. As my eldest was so traumatised, for a while I drove around in her car. I knew this was going to be a hard battle as I knew what sort of a man he was. As I said, the visits continued, and he tried to push for more and have a go with the supervisors, making out that he was the innocent one so that they felt sorry for him. They were not allowed to leave the centre, but I was horrified sometimes, when I went to pick them up, to find that he had taken them to his house and made them see his partner's children, promising them things if they lived with him, demanding to take them swimming, as I had to stop as they could not be supervised properly in those conditions and that would be his opportunity to have a go at my eldest. But he would also still play these little nasty mind games with my eldest. She was so bad the last time I collected her; she was crying and was sooo angry with me for allowing this to happen, breaking what she had made with him, and screaming, 'Mummy, I hate him! I don't want to see him any more. If I am made to, I am going to kill myself as it is not fair.' First thing on Monday morning, I put in an affidavit requesting that access be stopped as it was harming the girls. Fortunately the judge could see what damage it was doing, and he ruled that all visits be cancelled. That was after the girls had to see barristers and psychologists again, and they could see that he was doing these things but he was gladly and arrogantly denying it. The thing was people did not see or understand what he would do and there was no stopping him.

We had to go through very intense court sessions. They were awful and terrifying. I had to admit at times that I thought I cannot carry on; the girls were depending on me so much. What if I let them down?

It was very hard to sit there, listening to complete fabricated untruths, accusations, and allegations, and the audacity of this man—he would literally say and do anything to save himself. It also became very obvious that if you said or did anything against him, he would headhunt you and try and cause trouble for you or get you into trouble. He was very abusive in court and made so many bad lies about me. He would say things to me in the corridor, then deny them. He was so bad that one day, he threatened me and the girls and the barrister and we had to be ushered out of the fire exit for safety. The next time, he was so aggressive towards me in court and stormed out that the judge ruled that I had to have two security guards with me at all times when in court. It was so hard and frustrating, having to sit quietly and listen to all his nasty lies and not being able to do anything about it.

He abused all the barristers I had to represent me; it was so bad that no one would represent me in the end, so I had to find someone in desperation. Even the judges now could see what he was like and were very reluctant to take my case on. Also, if the judge did not give him the result he wanted, he would make personal complaints against them saying that they were lying and causing corruption in the court. And he accused them saying they were judges but had abused their legal authority and there was a misconduct of justice. The complaints never stopped, nor did the allegations. He even went to John Key and people in high places to lie and get support. I always remember him saying if you shout loud enough in the right high places you will get people listening to you. He even paraded outside John Key's office and burnt his flag in protest.

This was so overwhelming and offensive; it was the hardest part of my life. Something I never thought I would get through and survive. I saw him as this big monster. I wondered, 'How the hell am I going to make people see the truth when he is such a good liar and a bully?'

We were in court one day, and he stormed out in temper. That judge had ordered an assessment on him due to his outrageous behaviour. It came back that he had narcissistic personality disorder and he had seven out of ten categories, and anything over five was dangerous. So I suppose that was the start of people believing me that he had a serious problem and that he was dangerous and that he was unfit to see his daughters.

He started to lose his temper more and show his true colours. He also did the odd thing of breaking the protection order, but there was never any proof so they could not prosecute. He saw us in a mall one day. I calmly said to the girls, 'Quietly get up and walk out.' He just stood there with his feet apart arms folded, just staring at us, which was very intimidating. He then drove past their schools bang on home time, which terrified them when they saw him. I reported all of this, but he just denied it and played his silly games. So it was very much like hitting your head against a brick wall. Plus his partner would wrongfully back him all the way. The reason he gave for being outside their schools was that he had a puncture. The police did not believe him either, but they said they had no proof and there was nothing they could do. To prosecute, they had to have hard evidence, which he was so cleverly not providing. As I said, he was being exactly how I thought he would be, and I personally thought, 'How the hell can I compete with someone so devious as that?'

It was terrible in court as he would take snippets of my past life and make them into a terrible lie to the courts. My dad used to be a policeman; he lied and said my dad was thrown out of the police force. He made up all these nasty lies about my past. It was so hard to sit there and listen to his facetious lies. I couldn't believe he could stoop so low.

I was a nervous wreck. I was on so much medication to keep me calm and help me to deal with things. I am on high blood pressure tablets, because as soon as he comes into the equation, my blood pressure goes through the roof. And I really thought, 'I cannot go on, and this monster is never going to go away.'

Through all the nasty court appearances we had, he showed his true colours. The judge finally, thank God, believed me. Plus with all the evidence he had in front of him, he finally ruled that he was a dangerous man and that he was never to see the girls again for their safety and sanity and that if ever he breaks the protection order, it is to be dealt with very seriously, and that I was to have full custody of the children.

In desperation, he actually had one of the supervisors there, and he kept mouthing to her what to say; the judge saw this and warned him to stop. He just got angrier and more confused; hence why I said his mental health had taken a decline. I could not believe his audacity; he actually got his partner to say that he was like this because of his birth sign, and this was what they were like. The judge more or less told him that his partner was not doing him any good by saying silly things like that. But thankfully, the judge made up his own mind after seeing him in full swing and ruled that he was never to see the children, that all visits were permanently cancelled, and that he was a dangerous person. *Oh my god!* I couldn't believe this! They believed me; he hadn't fooled them; the truth did prevail! I had done it. I was in true shock and disbelief. Did this mean we could move on now and get on with our life without the fear of him trying to bully us or harm us?

Sadly, my mother died during all this nasty business, and he blocked us from going back to UK for the funeral and to pay our respects, which was hard on the girls as they loved their grandmother. Then last year, I had a call to say that my dad was not in good health and that he may not make it, so it was important that we go and see him. So we had to go to court to get the order lifted to enable us to go home for a visit after a two-day hearing—where he was aggressive and threatening to us all again and it ended up in him being tackled on the floor by three security guards and finally being arrested and taken away by the police. He also mouthed to me when everyone was busy reading the affidavits, '*I am going to kill you.*' I became very distressed. He obviously denied it, but the judge believed me as I became very distressed and was in a state of shock and panic. He went for me in court, and the judge ruled that he be taken away. He shouted and screamed, which was very distressing to me. I could not believe it had come to this and how bad he had become.

Due to this awful show of his aggression, the judge ruled that we could have our passports back and we were able to go back to UK to see our family. That was so emotional; he gave us a time for us to be back, which I had no problem with as I never intended in running away again anyway. So to my daughters' delight, we were able to go back and see our family, see my poorly father, and pay our respects to my mum's grave.

Since our return, we have never seen him again, thank goodness, but he did try and contact me via email, which I reported to the police. They arrested him and charged him due to having evidence; he was given six months to be good, which he obviously was, so he has been discharged with no conviction. I just hope that that is enough to make him realise that this is not a game and he is to leave us alone and let us get on with our lives, 'cause we certainly don't want to see him again. And we are now gladly divorced legally.

CHAPTER 5

Because the fear and trauma was so serious and dramatic, we ended up moving four times as the girls were convinced that he knew where we were living and we were going to die. The first house we lived in, my eldest was convinced that he knew where we were living. So she walked past our home every day after school to fool anyone who was watching. The last house we lived, there was a fire during the evening; we called the fire brigade as the house was full of smoke and smelt of burning and it was found to be an electrical fault under the house. We were very lucky that it had been smouldering for a long time and it was not far to bursting into flames. We were all really frightened and convinced that it was him. Also one night, my eldest was on the computer, and I had gone to bed. She came in as white as a ghost. She was shaking uncontrollably, convinced that her dad was at the window. I had to calm her down and reassure her he was not there. This affected them really badly, so we had to move shortly after as they were sure that he had come to carry out his threat. So now, for our safety, we are in a house in someone else's name, and the car is in someone else's name, so for the first time, we are feeling safe.

During all this process, he had a terrible effect on the girls. We have all been diagnosed with post-traumatic stress disorder; my eldest has suffered from anger, fear, and depression; I have had to put up with terrible anger outbursts, crying, depression, and terrible mood swings. It was hell trying to get her through it, but with help and support, she has come out the other side. In the end, she was so bad that the doctor recommended that she go on antidepressants, which she is now on and she is much better. Because for a while, the doctor was really quite worried about her as she was terribly distressed. She has stopped having bad dreams and terrible flashbacks. She also cannot read for a long time as her concentration level is very low. She has had intensive counselling, and thankfully, they have made her see through the bad and she has managed to put her dad away, so much so that he does not bother her again, although it still is such a huge disappointment.

Now my youngest is going through the same, which I must say is a huge drain and very tiring. She has no confidence, no motivation, and no enthusiasm; she hates men, is very close to me, and feels threatened very easily. She becomes very abusive also, and I feel very depressed, as she spends days in her pyjamas and doesn't want to do anything or go anywhere. She has no sense of humour and takes life very seriously. It is very easy to offend her. I am so worried about her, as I must say the psychologists used to say to me that I would be more worried about the youngest one as the quiet ones are the worst. My eldest used to lash out all the time and have huge temper outbursts; my youngest would do or say nothing. Now that she is growing older, she is coming out of it. I feel so sorry for her as she is hurting so much, and, I think, she feels lost and doesn't know what to do. I have got in touch with an organisation which was recommended to me, and I am going to try my hardest to help her and get her the right help so that she can deal with everything and manage to put it away and get on with her own life. Also due to my terrible childhood, I have learnt from that and made sure that I am an easy-going and approachable mum so that they can come and talk to me about everything and anything, including their wrong time of the month so that I know that they are OK and able to deal with anything in life. They come to me about anything.

I also am on so much medication to help me to cope with life and not fall apart. The other week, I had a mild stroke as my body was breaking down. I often feel like giving up, but I have to keep fighting on for the sake of my kids.

All I can say is that it has been a very hard battle, but for yourself and the sake of your children, you have to fight this and keep going as there is life at the end of the tunnel.

It has been horrific, and I never thought we would get through it. Having to deal with both girls' pain and anguish has been the hardest thing in my life, and as I said often, I have thought that life was never worth it.

This has left me with no confidence, and I am scared and vulnerable. I do not trust anyone and have no will to carry on, and I must say that if it wasn't for the girls, I don't think I would have carried on..

My eldest has had a lot of time off school as she has had a lot of flashbacks and panic attacks; she has had a lot of counselling, and, as I said with a good doctor, she has managed to come through it and is now able to accept her dad for what he is and know that she does not want to see him again.

My youngest is now going through it; she has been the quiet one, and everyone said, 'She is the one that you should most worry about.' She is very close to me and does not trust anyone. She is very shy, quiet, and sensitive, and she has no sense of humour and treats life very seriously, which breaks my heart. But I am sure that with the right help, we will get through it. I also am very hyper-vigilant, always looking for him in crowds; also, if I see his car or one like his, I immediately look at the registration number to check whether it is his car..

As I said near the beginning, my eldest had her dad throw a lighter at her eye and hurt her. Lately, we have had to have both their eyes tested due to their poor eyesight. They have diagnosed that her right eye pupil is damaged—at which he threw the lighter –and it has damaged her eyesight and she has to wear glasses. And she has very poor vision in that eye.

My youngest also has to wear glasses due to poor eyesight.

I also realised that my hearing was poor, so I went for a hearing test. Because of the things I reported that had gone on in my life and what my husband had done, I have very poor hearing and he has damaged it, so I now have use hearing aids due to the abuse and shouting he did to my ears.

If we go out, we are always on alert in case we see him, but I am hoping it will slowly ease off as time goes by. I have been in intensive therapy to help me to accept what has happened and be able to go ahead and live my life. I must say it has been slow and will continue to be so. But I will get there.

Also I never thought I could love and trust again, but I have met this amazing man who has stuck by me through thick and thin and who has stood by the trauma that both girls have suffered. He has allowed me to see that there are kind men out there who are genuine ready to give love and support unconditionally; it has taken me a long time to realise that, but I am finally there. I can honestly say that for the first time my girls are happy and actually enjoying life how one should. Seeing them happy makes me happy, and I must say, for the first time, it is nice to enjoy life and finally find love. Due to my lovely partner, we have a lovely home, the girls have their own possessions, and we have pets, after losing everything after running away from him. I must say that for me to have complete trust in my new partner and let some of my survival habits go away was not easy, but it is coming right. He understands, and I know it will get better after time. You know, the hardest thing is for me to actually believe that he loves me and that he thinks I am a good person. He does things for me like helping me do the washing, cooking, and looking after the kids, something I have always had to do on my own and survive with, but for the first time, I have someone who will help and share with me. Also what blows me away is that he brings me a cup of tea in bed! I have never had that, and it takes some getting used to. Also I think one of my faults is that I don't feel I am good enough to be treated like that. But I have been told that I have to believe in that, so I guess it will get better in time. I have a terrible habit; he pays me compliments, and I shoot him down immediately, laughing and saying, 'You need glasses,' or 'You can't see properly.'

I must admit this has changed me so much. I used to be really loving and romantic and would do anything with my partner, but since this has happened, I don't get excited about anything any more. I take each day as it comes. Also I am not particularly loving and romantic, in my own little way I suppose. I just haven't got it in me any more; plus I am hard and blunt. Also I like my own space now, and I am not going to give that up for anyone. I still share my life, but I still do things that I have fought for, like my independence and freedom, and actually have fun with my best friend—all things I have never been allowed to do. That is not meant in a nasty way; it is just where it has changed me. It is like this brick wall that has been built, and I am never going to put myself into that position ever again. I suppose I can say it has made me a lot stronger. And if you did this, you could do the same too. Just have to hang in there and go with what you believe in.

I feel so bad for my new partner as I know he wants more and sadly I cannot give it to him, so he needs a medal for hanging in there. I really wouldn't blame him if he wanted to walk away. I don't want him to, but I know that living with us is difficult at times, as all three of us have our own issues from the past and it is very hard..

Also my girls are getting through this. They have been through hell, and I never thought we would get there. But we have, and it has made everything worth it.

Also I am worried for my health as I need tablets to keep me calm, let me sleep, keep my blood pressure down, and keep me happy. This is all a repercussion of the past, but I am staying strong and hoping this will get better in time and hopefully will not have to have any medication. I also see a therapist; she is great. She has helped me heaps, but I know I am going to have to continue seeing her for a long time yet. I need help to move on, and I hope I can put all this behind me and enjoy some of my life. I must say I used to have nightmares and flashbacks all the time; thankfully, these have stopped now, so that is a great improvement.

This has also left me with no memory. I cannot remember anything, and I cannot concentrate or take anything in that anyone tells me. I also suffer from panic and anxiety attacks, but I know that with the right therapy and state of mind you can do this and you can conquer anything. So please don't sit back in your chair, saying, 'I can't so this. I am stuck'. You can do it, and you would never regret it. I cannot emphasise this enough. I know I was a coward for a very long time, but since I have done this, it has made me a much stronger person and I go for anything in life that is important.

So this leaves me one thing to say—follow your instincts, stand strong, and fight for what you believe in as there is light at the end of the tunnel and you can do it and finally to see your kids laugh and be happy; it makes it all worth it. You are a good person, and you deserve much better. I know you might not see it right now, but there is a Mr Right out there for you and the monster who is bullying you and abusing you right now is not the right one. You deserve better and you can get there. Believe in yourself, but, most importantly, tell yourself that your kids deserve a good start in life, not this abusive crap. So go on, be strong, and do whatever you have to do to get out of the situation. You can do it; believe in yourself.

All I can say is that I hope he continues to leave us alone and that we can finally enjoy life and hope that our health can improve as time goes by. And I also hope that reading this book really helps a lot of people to move on. I don't regret anything that I have done; it has made it all worth it, and, for the first time in my life, I have found proper life and happiness. Break that cycle. There is always someone out there for you who will help and advise. Good luck.